snapshot•picture library

TRACTORS

snapshot·picture·library

TRACTORS

FOG CITY PRESS

Published by Fog City Press,
a division of Weldon Owen Inc.
415 Jackson Street
San Francisco, CA 94111 USA
www.weldonowen.com

WELDON OWEN INC.
Group Publisher, Bonnier Publishing Group John Owen
Chief Executive Officer and President Terry Newell
Senior Vice President, International Sales Stuart Laurence
Vice President, Sales and New Business Development Amy Kaneko
Vice President, Publisher Roger Shaw
Executive Editor Elizabeth Dougherty
Assistant Editor Sarah Gurman
Associate Creative Director Kelly Booth
Senior Designer William Mack
Production Director Chris Hemesath
Production Manager Michelle Duggan
Color Manager Teri Bell

A WELDON OWEN PRODUCTION
© 2009 Weldon Owen Inc.

Library of Congress Control Number: 2009924572

ISBN-13: 978-1-74089-996-3

10 9 8 7 6 5 4 3 2 1
2009 2010 2011 2012

Printed by Tien Wah Press in Singapore.

Tractors are big, tough vehicles. Their main job is to pull heavy things. While they are not very fast, they are very powerful. They can drive on rugged ground and slippery slopes.

Tractors are perfect for working on farms. They pull machines that plow fields and sow seeds, work that horses used to do. But tractors also have other uses. You can find them on the beach pulling boats or in the mountains clearing snow.

Tractors are rugged, with large wheels and powerful engines.

Most tractors
have big wheels
at the back and
smaller ones
at the front.

Four-wheel
drive tractors
have bumpy
front tires.

It's easy to spot a two-wheel drive tractor. The front tires are much smoother.

A tractor's engine is at the front. It has an exhaust pipe that sticks up in the air.

At the back is a hitch. This lets you attach a tool or trailer to the tractor.

An attachment called a "harrow" is a farming tool that breaks up soil.

Tractors often pull trailers or wagons filled with useful items, such as crops or straw bales.

Tractors can tow other things, too. The blue tractor has an attachment to smooth the rodeo arena.

Some tractors can lift heavy items with arms called "loaders." These attach at the sides of the engine.

Farmers use
tractors for
all kinds of
jobs around
the farm.

The green tractor is applying chemicals to the soil, while the blue tractor is chopping grass into a wagon.

Some tractors carry hay bales. Others spread manure to fertilize the fields.

Tractors plow fields to help get them ready for planting crops.

After plowing, a tractor breaks up the soil using a harrow. The round blades on a harrow are called "disks."

To plant seeds, the tractor pulls a tool that sows the seeds in long, narrow rows.

Plants may be sprayed with a fertilizer to help them grow or a pesticide to stop insects from eating them.

When the crop is ready, a combine harvester cuts off the plants and cleans the grain. A tractor collects the grain in a wagon.

Tractors help
collect crops,
such as sugar
cane or corn.

Tractors can power machines called "balers" that make bales of straw and hay.

Not all tractors are used on farms. Some do jobs such as carrying logs or clearing snow.

These tractors work near the beach. They push boats into the water and then pull them out later.

Tractors are
hard-working
machines
that can do
many things.

You might see some tractors mowing grass in a park or backyard near your house.

You might see
some tractors
that are too
old and rusty
to work out
in the fields.

Old tractors were powered by steam. Some people enjoy restoring these tractors.

Tractors do
all sorts of jobs.
What have you
seen a tractor do?

Four-wheel drive tractor

In a four-wheel drive tractor, the engine powers all four wheels. The front wheels are almost as big as the back wheels, and they have thick, bumpy tires.

Two-wheel drive tractor

In a two-wheel drive tractor, the engine powers only the back wheels. The front tires are smooth and smaller than the back ones.

Engine

A tractor's engine is at the front. Because tractors often have to pull heavy loads, their engines are very big and powerful—and make a lot of noise!

Hitch

Tractors have hitches at the back for attaching trailers, baling machines, and tools such as plows and harrows. You can also attach other vehicles.

Tractor and trailer

Trailers are used for carrying things, such as harvested crops. Tractors can pull large trailers, even when they are completely full.

Loader

Some tractors have arms called "loaders" to lift things up. This tractor has a spiked tool at the end of its loader for lifting hay and straw bales.

Plow

A tractor can pull a plow to break up big blocks of earth and turn over the soil. Plowing helps to prepare the ground for planting new crops.

Harrow

After plowing, a tractor can pull a tool called a harrow over the soil. This makes the surface of the soil smooth, so new crops can be planted.

Baler

Tractors can also pull machines that pick up hay or straw and pack them into bales. The bales can be different shapes, including square, oblong, or round.

Snow blower

In winter, tractors are often used to clear snow off roads. A snow plow on the front of the tractor collects the snow, and a blower removes it.

Lawn mower

A ride-on mower is a small tractor with a lawn mower attached to the bottom. It can mow large areas of grass much more quickly than a hand-push lawn mower.

Steam tractor

The first tractors used coal as fuel. Burning the coal made steam, which drove the engine. This is also how the first trains worked.

ACKNOWLEDGMENTS

Weldon Owen would like to thank the staff at
Toucan Books Ltd, London, for their assistance
in the production of this book: Daniel Gilpin,
Author and Researcher; Ellen Dupont, Project
Manager; and Carol Davis, Designer.
For Flynn, a boy who loves tractors!